# AUTHENTIC LEADERSHIP

## A PRIMER FOR PROFESSIONALS AND SMALL BUSINESS OWNERS

# DR. BILL CAMPBELL
# &
# DR. DAVE NIBOUAR

# Prologue

## The Velveteen Rabbit Revisited

By Jim McKelvey

I recently came upon this little excerpt from the story of *The Velveteen Rabbit* by Margery Williams. I remembered it as a child's story, but upon re-reading it I found a story for grownups too.

"The Skin Horse had lived longer in the nursery than any of the others. He was so old that his brown coat was bald in patches and showed the seams underneath, and most of the hairs in his tail had been pulled out to string bead necklaces. He was wise, for he had seen a long succession of mechanical toys arrive to boast and swagger, and by and by break their mainsprings and pass away and he knew that they were only toys, and would never turn into anything else. For nursery magic is very strange and wonderful, and only those playthings that are old and wise and experienced like the Skin Horse understand all about it.

"What is Real?" asked the Rabbit one day, when they were lying side by side near the nursery fender, before Nana came to tidy the room. "Does it mean having things that buzz inside you and a stick-out-handle?"

"Real isn't how you are made," said the Skin Horse. "It's a thing that happens to you. When a child loves you for a long, long time, not just to play with, but really loves you, then you become Real."

"Does it hurt?" asked the Rabbit.

"Sometimes," said the Skin Horse, for he was always truthful. "When you are Real you don't mind being hurt."

"Does it happen all at once, like being wound up?" he asked. "Or bit by bit?"

"It doesn't happen all at once," said the Skin Horse. "You become. It takes a long time. That's why it doesn't often happen to people who break easily, or have sharp edges, or who have to be carefully kept. Generally, by the time you are Real, most of your fur has been loved off, your eyes drop out and you get loose in the joints and very shabby. But these things don't matter at all, because once you are Real you can't be ugly, except to people who don't understand."

*Margery Williams*

The story, of course, is about becoming "Real." In this case, it tells how toys sometimes become Real by virtue of the steadfast love of a child, and about how the toy gets worn out by being so fiercely loved over a long time.

Have you ever had a toy, a doll or other precious belonging that became "loose in the joints," or worn thin where the paint or fur was loved away? What if we opened ourselves to being that well used? What if we opened ourselves to the love of friends, family, clients and co-workers?

We could become more Real by letting the love affect us...letting it touch us more deeply. What a blessing it could be to allow the love in and to become more Real in all of our relationships...to allow the love of others to rub off our fur, and the hugs to make us loose in the joints. Sure it could hurt, but "when you are Real you don't mind being hurt." (My own experience from forty years in dental practice, forty years of married life and sixty-five years of living suggests that the plusses outweigh the minuses.)

So, let's open the heart door, let people care for us, care about us and love us. Let's give up being carefully kept, give up our fragile parts and our sharp edges. Let's join the velveteen rabbit and become more REAL.

✲ ✲ ✲

*Jim McKelvey is a retired dentist living in Newark, DE with his wife, Carol, two cats and a dog. He is a long-time member of the Emeritus Retreat Group, from which much of the material in this book was derived. Sixty-five years of living have sanded off his rough edges and made him about as authentic as a person can be.*

# INTRODUCTION

**Dr. Bill Campbell**

In my 40 years of consulting with businesses of all kinds, I have discovered there are great differences between small, private, service oriented businesses and large corporate organizations. Much of the leadership and management literature in recent years is technique oriented, specifically designed for survival and effectiveness in large organizations. While these ideas might be applicable in a management-heavy corporate structure, they simply do not apply to running a small business. The small business owner/professional simply doesn't have the time to produce revenue and lead the team, and doesn't have the training to implement and follow up on complex management strategies. Unless the technique-oriented material is simple, understandable and specifically geared to the small business, it just doesn't get used.

This book is designed for any professional who is the chief producer, C.E.O., C.O.O., C.F.O., leader, marketer, human resource specialist, business development manager and cleaning person for his or her business. It is intended for medical offices, law offices, dental offices, veterinary clinics, CPAs,

> **Many of the skills that are useful to large corporations do not work for leaders of small businesses.**

beauty boutiques, consultants, psychologists, architects – any service-oriented organization where the professional is a significant revenue producer and also the leader.

> **Private practices generally run more like a family than a corporation.**

The last ten years of my practice have been devoted to helping my professional colleagues with their leadership issues within the context of their own organization. Let's face it. We are trained as providers of our own "magic," whatever that may be. We are not trained to run a business dealing with staff issues, develop marketing strategies, or be efficient money managers, human resources experts or property managers.

Most of my clients say: "If I could just practice my profession and deal with my clients or patients, I would be a happy camper." The truth is you can't **just** practice, you must also lead, and that is the reason for this book.

As I wind down my career, I want to leave behind some of the learning and experiences I have lived in 40 years of leadership focus. I've concluded that leaders of small

> **Our society needs authentic leaders.**

businesses are most effective when they are authentic and true to their unique basic natures. In other words, the most effective practices are those that reflect the "realness" of the leader. The congruence of the real self of the professional with the operation of the business is the key to success and, perhaps more significant, one of the keys to happiness.

So this book will be short and sweet. It's about finding your authentic self that has been buried for years under the pressures of a protracted graduate school education, establishment of a business, the need to make a living, the trials and tribulations of adulthood, and most important, the unrealistic expectations we place on ourselves every minute of every working day.     WSC

> **There is a huge difference between management and leadership.**

## Dr. Dave Nibouar

Every consultant needs a client. That's where I come in. I first met Bill in the mid-nineties through a national organization that provided business and leadership advice for dentists. With the help of this organization I had learned to apply simple business principles to my practice, an aspect of my education that was simply not addressed in dental school. From a business perspective my numbers were above average and I was a financial success, yet I did not FEEL successful. Looking back, it's obvious that I was the poster child for what has been called the "failure of success." Eventually, I began to see that the business approach, although valuable, did not address the real problem. Somehow, in my quest for what I thought was success, I had been aiming at the wrong target and lost myself in the process.

> **The fundamental choice is to be happy, no matter what.**

Some years before I met Bill, I had formed a small retreat group with similarly challenged colleagues. We were "on the path," although I'm not sure we knew exactly which path we were on. All we knew for sure was that the path we had taken up until then was not getting us to where we wanted to be. I invited Bill to join the group. We needed his psychological expertise and he needed access to our dysfunctional dental practices.

Working with Bill, I have come to understand how I got myself into this situation and have largely managed to claw myself out of it. Bill has come to understand the strange, almost ubiquitous dysfunction that affects most professionals/small business owners and has managed to put it into an understandable and usable context. I think it's accurate to say that we have spent the last ten years learning from one another.

Bill is primarily responsible for the existence of this book. I'm flattered that he asked me to contribute, knowing that he would get a lot more feedback from me than perhaps he was ready for. My contributions come from two perspectives: First, more than thirty-five years of experience in the trenches and second, from the years of independent reading and research I've done in an attempt to figure out which "universal truths" I have ignored or violated in my journey along the pot-holed road of life.

All of this has convinced me of several things. First, there ARE universal truths and it is our job to discover them. When we do, it will seem as if we were the first to ever see the light. But the more studying you do, the more you will be surprised to find that the things that seemed like a revelation to you were discovered in the mists of antiquity. They may have been described in different terminology or used a different metaphor, but the core stuff is ancient wisdom that doesn't change.

Second, it's easy for me to see how other people shoot themselves in the foot in their own lives but virtually impossible to see how I do it to myself. It was a struggle for

> **The service you have been trained to deliver is not nearly as important to the success of your business as the way you take care of your client/patient.**

me to get to the point where I could believe Bill's reports about the antics that were occurring right under my nose in my own practice, let alone accept the information and act on it.

Third, a small business or professional practice is ALWAYS a reflection of the leader. That is not necessarily good news and is particularly hard to swallow when you come to realize that you are presiding over

> **If your professional life isn't fun, you'll burn out in the long haul.**

a dysfunctional business. If the business is dysfunctional and I'm the leader then. . .                                         DBN

# CHAPTER 1: WHAT DO YOU WANT TO BE WHEN YOU GROW UP?

Who said being a "grownup" is desirable anyway? If you think about it, our most endearing and desirable human traits belong to the kid in all of us. I wouldn't trade the wonder, the passion, the openness, the honesty, the humor, the curiosity, and the fun of being a kid for all of the supposed rewards of adulthood.

Being a <u>real</u> leader involves a process of identifying and unlearning the phoniness, the righteousness, the rigidity and, above all, the seriousness that we learned on the road to becoming a grownup. The most successful practices I work with have the most fun!

There's an idea implicit in "what do you want to be when you grow up?" that is often misunderstood. Most parents, teachers, religious leaders, and business people really mean "what do you want to <u>do</u> when you grow up?"

**You are not what you do.**

Doing and being are two different animals. Most grownups have lost sight of what it means to <u>be</u>. Adults define themselves and others by what they do, not by who they are. "My son is a proctologist." "I scored an eagle on the 16<sup>th</sup> hole." "I'm a history major." "I'm the past president of the Order of Chipmunks." "Doing" is the measuring stick in our society. What is important to adults in our society is your title, your bank account, your golf handicap, your I.Q. Who you <u>are</u> gets lost.

Children, on the other hand, define themselves and others by their state of being. "Doctor" tells nothing about the quality of the person, how much fun this person has, how passionate he is about his practice, or how much compassionate energy he expends with each client or patient on a daily basis. His title only gives his pedigree. Children perceive adults on the basis of what they sense about the person; their smile, their warmth, their touch and openness to the child's innocence.

**You are not your image.**

In my own case, the expectations were set very early in my life for what the adults wanted me to be when I grew up. I was raised in a medically oriented family where my grandfather was a dentist and my mom was a microbiologist, so naturally I was going to be a doctor (if I could survive the seriousness of growing up.) The complication was that my Dad was an all-conference football hero who played in the pros for three years before he was injured. Like any "good" kid, I incorporated the expectations of both parents. In my innocence, I imagined that I was going to be a professional football player on weekends while I practiced medicine during the week. I was well into my undergraduate studies before I realized that those conflicting expectations weren't in the cards.

My wife grew up in a sales oriented family. Her dad programmed "retail" into her expectations very early. As a young teen she worked as a sales person in a women's clothing store, went to Michigan State for a two year retailing program and bought into those expectations until she transferred in her junior year and fell in love with literature and writing. Ultimately, she became head of a high school English Department rather than a V.P. at Neiman Marcus.

These personal stories are included to illustrate how strong parental, societal and educational expectations push us into choices that make us grow up into serious,

> **You can never <u>do</u> enough to feel worthy.**

often dysfunctional, and sometimes miserable "human doings."

Now that I have the benefit of 40 years of perspective on being a grownup, the world looks a lot different than it did when I was a child. What I want to be when I grow up is curious, fearless, open, honest, humorous, peaceful and loving. What I want to do when I grow up is to play golf, walk my dog, travel with my wife, write books and work with my clients to become more authentic myself. Does that make me an authentic leader? I don't know. That's for others to say, but I do know that it's very satisfying being me these days.

How about you? Now that you have put so much time and effort into

> **If you focus on your limitations and listen to constructive criticism, you will always sabotage yourself.**

becoming a serious, grownup professional, how do you like yourself and your business? Does your work provide you with joy? Are you happy?

If you are like most of my clients, the answer would <u>not</u> be a resounding "yes!" It appears that in

> **Worry is the 8<sup>th</sup> deadly sin.**

order to become a professional in this society, we must become something other than our authentic self. Surviving the long haul of

3

education, starting a business when you don't know how, establishing a clientele, buying a home, paying off student loans and stepping on loaded diapers doesn't leave much energy for being yourself. After they have climbed the mountain of expectations to become adult professionals, the clients in my practice frequently ask, "Is that all there is?" Or they might say: "I don't really know who I am any more. Whatever happened to that spontaneous, open and honest kid that inhabited this body so many years ago? What happened to that joyous child? How did I become this tired, worried, serious grownup?"

Some call this a mid-life crisis. I call it the "failure of success." (I actually borrowed this term from Dan Baker, author of the book <u>What Happy People Know</u>.) It is extremely difficult to create any kind of balance in a life that demands so much of our energy and focus just to survive all the hoops we must jump through to become a professional. Most of my clients are well into their forties before they start to become aware of the toll this professional survival mode has taken on their humanity and their health/peace of mind.

> **It's impossible to be tense and relaxed at the same time.**

In terms of leadership, I would speculate that most professionals' leadership strategy, if they have one at all, is based on fear of survival. We are bottom line oriented because we've been taught that it is the way we keep score in our society and the pressure associated with that orientation makes us model anxiety, seriousness, righteousness and rigidity. It takes a conscious effort for us to find the energy to crank up real caring for our clients or patients. There is no real healing energy left for our clients; it's used up by the burdens of being a serious professional.

Not a pretty picture? We haven't even mentioned what our personal and home lives are really like! So what's the answer to all this? It's very simple but it's not easy. The reality is that you have become an adult, albeit an unhappy one. Becoming aware of the fear based behaviors that have made you a "successful" professional is a big step in recapturing your natural, authentic, child-like perceptions once again.

> **Authenticity is an inside-out process.**

Buried beneath those adult, fear based behaviors are the childlike qualities that are the key to being happy. They are just lost in the struggles of the past. You <u>can</u> choose to change the rules of this serious game and rediscover the real person behind the wall of degrees, plaques of contributions to your profession and the shingle on the door to your office. In my experience, the behavior and focus that got you to adulthood, professionalism and being grown up will destroy your life if you continue to use them to chase after the success you have had in the past. The good news is that same focus, if applied in a more healthy direction, can lead you back to your natural self. Businesses that reflect the true nature of the professional are the ones that thrive and enrich everyone associated with them. Professionals, staff and clients/patients all benefit from a leadership formula that comes from the heart and soul of the leader. Naturalness, realness and authenticity become the engine for your train. The trick is to keep it on the right track because there is nothing as sad and wasteful as the failure of success! So the answer to "what do you want to be when you grow up?" is not a doctor, a dentist or a lawyer. It's "just plain ME"!

# CHAPTER 2:
# SCHOOL DAYS

My first professional job was teaching 6th graders. Fresh out of college, my passion was to help these young minds and bodies

**You demonstrate learning by changing your behavior.**

develop and grow using the techniques I learned as an undergraduate in the school of education. I grew up with the idea that school meant mastery of the 3 Rs - readin', writin' and 'rithmetic - but I soon discovered that the real agenda of schools is to civilize those "wild beasts" called children.

My idea that my job was actually to teach these kids something was at odds with my colleagues' notion of

**Children can be our greatest teachers if we stop trying to "raise" them and learn to listen.**

what constitutes education, and was certainly not in sync with the principal of the school. In very short order, I learned that what was really important to the adults was that I maintained control in the classroom. I

was expected to become a kind of Marine drill instructor, lining up and marching the kids to lunch, to recess, or to the bathroom. I soon realized that recess was the only time that the children really learned anything worthwhile because they were free of adult supervision and control.

My own educational experience was an example of learning to "play the game" of meeting the teachers and coaches expectations.  The kids in my classes who were best at playing the game were considered the bright and clever ones, while those who couldn't or wouldn't play the game were labeled as slow, disruptive, rebellious, or just plain dumb.

I think the reason that I went into education in the first place was to revolutionize the system of adult expectations. It's ironic that here I am at almost 70 years of age trying to do the same thing with grown professionals who need to recapture the spontaneity that came naturally to them in the 6th grade. What happened to that spontaneity? Where did it go? Why wasn't recess more important to the grownups at my school?

The authentic educator in me knows that the educational process has a lot of different aspects. Most people think that education is all about stuffing facts into young brains. That's mastery of the "three r's" and it's the official agenda of education, but I would suggest that it's not the most significant part. The trouble starts when we get into the hidden agenda of education – civilizing the wild beasts called children.

A good way to look at this is to make a distinction between teaching and learning. They are two different processes. In teaching, the presenter is in charge of the curriculum (the "three r's") and also the context in which the curriculum is presented. The presenter can easily measure the student's success in mastering the curriculum by objective testing. If the curriculum is "rithmetic" and the student gains the ability to correctly spit out the multiplication tables, the teaching process has succeeded. But in order for success to occur, the presenter has to create and control the context where the student can take in the information. The uncivilized little beast has to learn to comply with the context. That's part of the civilizing process. The teacher defines the behavior the student must exhibit to be in compliance with the expectations and perceptions of the teacher. In order to be compliant, the student must abandon his/her natural, but probably wild, approach to the learning task and instead try to please the teacher. This form of teaching is what most of us experienced from kindergarten through our advanced degrees. We became good students; we learned to comply with the expectations of the adult world; we became civilized. It's the necessary, albeit hidden, agenda of the educational system. But somehow we lost our authenticity in the process. How did this happen?

What we have just examined is education from the teacher's perspective. Learning, on the other hand, is education from the student's perspective. A student is like a sponge and takes in everything coming at him, including the curriculum (the three r's), compliance with the context set by the teacher _and_ all the hidden attitudes and prejudices that the teacher subconsciously transmits. There's a built-in conflict between the teacher's desire for compliance and the student's tendency to experiment and try to develop in his own way. The student's whole brain _and_ body are involved. If the teacher respects the student's natural inclinations rather than inhibiting them, it can be a chaotic, messy, out of control process. Teachers that are truly facilitators of learning must understand the difference between the student's <u>behavior</u> and the student himself.

In the first chapter we took a quick peek at the distinction between being and doing. The student's behavior is a "doing". The student himself is a "being". The true facilitator of learning understands the difference and knows how to simultaneously VALUE THE PERSON AND CRITICIZE THE BEHAVIOR. This kind of teacher has a high tolerance for trial and error. There is no such thing as a mistake, only learning. The teacher in this model will guide the discovery of the student, but his primary goal is not compliance; it is to encourage experimentation with subject matter and context to develop the natural strengths of the learner. Such a process encourages learners to discover what they do well and then make it better! This same model applies to the authentic leader. Real leaders play to everyone's strengths. Their real task is to create an environment where everyone they touch can become a better human being.

> **Nurturing authentic children may be your biggest contribution and gift to the world.**

### *Freedom*

*He was born a survivor.*

*The holocaust horror and fear was "normal"*

*for this joyous, creative little boy.*

*It was all he had ever known.*

*He always had this nagging feeling*

*that something was very wrong*

*and that somehow it was his responsibility*

*to make everything right. . .to fix the suffering.*

*So he became the caregiver to his wounded, emotionally broken family.*

*He chose to exchange his childhood for the burden*

*of being responsible, to administer to everyone's need and pain.*

*A heavy load for a twelve year old.*

*Head of the family's business, welfare,*

*and responsible for everyone's feelings.*

*All encompassing!*

*Overwhelming!*

*And he pulled it off!*

*He made a career out of caring.*

*He extended his responsibility to his patients,*

*his family, his staff, and the entire community.*

*After all, that's his legacy.*

*Then as an adult, he found a mentor*

*who gave him permission to rediscover that creative little boy.*

*He gave himself permission to*

*put down his burden and pick up his sketch pad.*

*Now he remembers the past*

*as a strange sort of blessing.*

*Now he can choose to remember the story of
where he came from*

*without the burden of having to make it go away.*

*He can remember the roots of his being*

*without the feeling that he in any way*

*needs to feel responsible for fixing it.*

*FREEDOM!*

*You are a miracle, Isaac.*

*Bill Campbell*

Most of us grown up professionals haven't had this kind of learning experience, or if we did, it was at the hands of that very special teacher/leader/mentor that we will never forget because he/she was interested in the development of our being, not in playing the compliance game.

> **Complying with other people's expectations becomes a debilitating habit.**

It is no wonder that we have forgotten what it is like to be authentic, because in order to survive and succeed in an educational system that rewards compliance, we lose track of who we really are. Compliance demands that we try to become somebody else – somebody that exists only in the expectations of the adults that we are trying so desperately to please. And when the adult doing the teaching doesn't understand the difference between the student's problematic "doing" and his valuable, wonderful, lovable "being," authenticity goes down the drain. Instead of learning that he is just fine but his behavior could be improved, the student decides that, "I'M NO GOOD. I'M WORTHLESS. I'LL NEVER MEASURE UP".

### ***Learned Degree***

*I had a friend ask me once,*
*When was the last time you failed?*

*Have you ever turned left at a fork*
*When right, you could have prevailed?*

*I stopped and pondered this question*
*And how much time she could spend.*

*I started listing my failures*
*From childhood to last weekend.*

*As I announced my shortcomings,*
*And my failure to earn a degree,*

*I stopped rather abruptly-*
*Without them I wouldn't be ME!*

*I wouldn't have met my soul mate*
*If it weren't for these "mistakes."*

*I wouldn't have climbed a mountain*
*Or paddled a Northwoods lake.*

*I can't imagine life without*
*My mountain log cabin dream*

*If I chose a corporate ladder*
*Over rising above with a team.*

*So to answer my friend's question,*
*Failure is a state of mind.*

*We may choose a different road*
*That will leave us a tad behind.*

*That doesn't mean you're a failure,*
*When doors close, a window you'll see.*

*And if not for "unwise" choices,*
*I wouldn't have learned this degree.*

*Sharon Baird  August 2001*
*Office Manager Limestone Dental*

It might seem as if this chapter is intended as a scathing indictment of the educational system. That's not completely true. The destruction of our natural selves actually started before we came in contact with the school system. Mom and Dad had a big hand in it, as did the environment in which we spent our early years. And here's a big news flash - it's not a result of somebody screwing up. The loss, and potential for subsequent recovery, of our authentic selves is built into our development. It's a natural, unavoidable part of being human. It's documented in mythology, fairy tales, legends, poems and religious parables. And since we can't avoid it, let's look at a "Cliff's Notes" version of human development so we can understand how our disintegration into pathetic, happiness-challenged professionals fits into the great scheme of things.

A human being begins life completely fused to the environment. Technically speaking, the first nine months are spent as an anatomical part of the mother. At birth, the baby emerges as a separate organism but is still totally dependent upon the environment for survival. In fact, it takes many months before the baby even becomes aware that it exists as a physical entity apart from Mom and the environment. From that point on, human development is the story of increasing physical and emotional differentiation from the rest of the world. This is, of course, an extremely complex process with many opportunities for things to go wrong, but ultimately, somewhere between the ages of six and ten, the child develops the understanding that he is a completely separate physical and emotional being. This realization is invariably a big pothole in the road of life for the child. Think about this from the perspective of the evolving child; if the child cries at six months, the world (Mom, Dad, Grandma, etc.) responds to make everything better. In a sense, the child controls the world. At three or four years, warm hugs come from Grandma just because the child "is." The child's four-year-old awareness has evolved enough to understand that just "being" is enough. By age six or seven, the world looks a lot bigger to the child. Now there are a lot more expectations and complications. Somewhere along the line, the child comes to understand that he is a separate entity in the world and that, in order to survive and prosper, the world expects some behavioral changes. The child learns that, in the eyes of the world, he's not perfect.

The point is no one escapes this lesson. It's not a defect in the great scheme of things. It's not because your parents screwed up. It's reality. Because of the nature of our own human development, every one of us translates the news that we are not perfect into some variation or combination of the two primal fears – "I'm not enough" and/or "something awful is going to happen." Like Adam and Eve, we lived the beginning of our lives in a sort of Garden of Eden. And also like Adam and Eve, we got kicked out. We have all been wounded. Somewhere along the line, life poked a hole in us and our spontaneous, authentic self leaked out.

The question, then, is not whether or not we were wounded. That's a condition of existence. The real question is whether or not the wound has healed. In a perfect world, every teenager would spend time with an authentic adult – a mentor who honored his being and knew how to "honor the person and criticize the behavior." The kid would learn that he was, in fact, a valuable human being and that he was capable of coping with whatever awful things might happen. In other words, the wounded teenager would heal and become a happy, authentic adult. Unfortunately, we don't live in a perfect world and authentic mentors are in short supply. Teachers are in a perfect position to heal the wound, but a teacher that has not been healed himself can only perpetuate it. This is particularly true in professional schools where the faculty is often teaching because their own fears are disabling enough to make them ineffective in the "real world" of private practice.

Given the reality described above, the "failure of success" becomes a lot more understandable. An unhealed wound is an uncomfortable thing and kids usually try to deal with the pain by using one of three general strategies.

One group gives up, sinks under the weight of it, and becomes chronic underachievers. They often get caught up in addictions. These kids don't make it to professional school. Some of them don't even make it to adulthood.

Another group sort of gets lost in the wound. We refer to them, and they think of themselves, as victims. In a very real sense, their wound becomes their identity.

> **Victimhood is based on the idea that you don't have a choice.**

If you have gotten this far in this book, you belong with me in the third group. We're the overachievers. We mask our underlying sense of worthlessness by trying harder, doing more and doing better. We often become perfectionists, and it seems perfectly sensible to us to try to enforce perfection on an inherently imperfect world. Doing our best is not good enough; we've got to be perfect. We accumulate impressive collections of certificates on the wall and long strings of letters after our names. The problem is that we are trying to heal a defect in our being with an excess of doing and the attempted cure, although it looks admirable to the outside world, doesn't address the disease.

There are as many fascinating combinations and variations of these three coping strategies as there are wounded people. But they all result in the inner emptiness, joylessness and lack of authenticity that we, dear readers, have come to experience as the "failure of success."

The bottom line is this: we are FEAR-BASED. The certificates on the wall, the respected professional practice, the McMansion in the suburbs and the Mercedes have not quieted the little voice buried deep inside us that keeps whispering, "You're not good enough. Your colleagues are doing better than you. If you don't get everything perfect, something awful is going to happen. Face it, friend. You're WORTHLESS."

So, you might say, if all this unhappiness is the just the result of things that happened to me as I was growing up and learning the wrong thing from my experiences, can't I just somehow "unlearn" it? Well, the idea of unlearning this stuff is a simple concept, but actually doing it is very difficult because of the years of conditioned compliance we all have been exposed to and the deeply buried attitude of worthlessness that has resulted. We have actually become hard-wired to believe - and behave - as if this myth about worthlessness were true. Despite what you may have come to believe, I don't think that you are worthless or that your real self is a wild beast that will rape and pillage if allowed to surface. I'm merely pointing out that we have been playing by the wrong rules about how to "make it" in this competitive professional world for so long that it's not easy to find the joyful, curious, loving creature that lives under this façade of adult professionalism.

You might well be sitting there reading this and saying to yourself, "Hah! That worthlessness and fear stuff obviously applies to some of my colleagues, but it certainly doesn't apply to me! I'm not afraid of anything." Really? Ask yourself the questions below. How many of them make you squirm a

> **Bravado and arrogance are covers for a fear-based person.**

little? If you are able to come up with answers, how do you feel about them? A little bit sheepish? Or maybe even a little ashamed?

- When's the last time you laughed until you cried?
- When's the last time you were naughty?
- When's the last time you played a joke on someone?
- When's the last time you were silly?
- When's the last time you were inappropriate?
- When's the last time you did something truly spontaneous?
- When's the last time you got dirty on purpose?
- When's the last time you did a somersault?
- When's the last time you played jacks or hopscotch?
- When's the last time you jumped rope or played dodge ball?
- When's the last time you really didn't give a rip how you were dressed or how you looked?
- When's the last time you broke something just for the hell of it?
- When's the last time you thought about what kind of a kid you were?
- How old were you when you gave up being a kid and decided to grow up?
- How old were you when you consciously contemplated "what do I want to be when I grow up?"
- When's the last time you cried when you were happy?
- When's the last time you unconditionally felt whole and happy?

It might seem like I'm encouraging you to regress into childhood and forget being an adult. Well, that's really not true. I'm suggesting that in order for you to become a real leader, to function from your authentic self, you need to restore <u>balance</u> in your life. The adult survival skills you have developed are very useful when you need them, but it's not healthy to live as if everything is "life and death." The key to lightening up is to remember what you were like before you decided to be "somebody." Being a very successful yet miserable S.O.B. feels lousy and it's just plain bad business!

### ***The Evil Gremlin***

*Something is casting*
*Shadows on my soul.*
*The Evil Gremlin*
*Dragged me in her hole.*

*She fills me with lies*
*That keep me confused.*
*My spirit faded*
*So pale, badly bruised.*

*Kept in the shadow*
*Of my soul from where*
*My true voice is heard,*
*But I'll seldom share.*

*Keep burning sunshine*
*To brighten my way.*
*This Gremlin, I'm sure,*
*Will not go away.*

*But I know she's there,*
*She can be a snake.*
*Off guard, unprepared,*
*I'll be hers to take.*

*Back into her cave*
*Of deceit and pain,*
*She'll try to damage*
*My spirit again.*

*But I know who she's*
*Pretending to be,*
*She'll have a hard time*
*To try and beat me.*

*Sharon Baird   November 2001*

# CHAPTER 3:
# THE JOURNEY

> **There is no one way to do anything.**

The process of discovering your authentic self is always unique to you. Every real person has a story, most often stranger than fiction. I can't tell you what your trip has been up to now or will be in the future, but I can describe some steps that seem common to most of the travelers on this road.

In the first chapters, I explained how children differentiate from their environment, go through the process of being civilized, are taught to be compliant, get wounded, somehow survive our educational system and then settle into "serious" professional adulthood.

So, let's pick it up right there at adulthood. Most folks try very hard to be responsible and civilized grownups. Most of us marry or settle into a relationship. We start some kind of career. We might choose to have 2.3 children. We probably acquire a mortgage, credit card debt, pay taxes, and maybe have a divorce or split-up or two. We learn to take all of this very seriously. We work hard all week. We recover on weekends or an occasional vacation. Some of us medicate ourselves to survive day to day. Others get lost in the unreality of "reality" shows, professional sports or computer games. We become reactors rather than actors on our own stage of life. We forget the fun of taking chances that we experienced as kids. We learn to play it "safe" and view any kind of risk as something to be avoided. The responsible adult retreats into fear of getting hurt.

Then one day we wake up and think, "Something is horribly wrong here. Is this all there is to life? Do I really have fun anymore, or do I just medicate myself into believing I'm enjoying life? What's real here? I've done all I'm supposed to have done and still I feel lonely and isolated. I feel empty. I feel tired, but I'm supposed to feel good. Look at all I've done! I am "somebody" in this community. I serve people in my business. I'm active in the church and at my club. I've got a great spouse/partner and my kids are doing okay. I'm slowly getting out of debt. I'm making progress, damn it! Then why do I feel so empty? So isolated? I work so hard. For what?"

> **You are only as good as your habits.**

Alcoholics call this condition the "bottom." The first step in their recovery is acceptance of the fact that they are powerless over the effects of alcohol. In my experience, it's the same for burned out professional folks. We have to accept that our formula for survival and success isn't really working so well and that we have trapped ourselves by thinking we can't change it. We need to accept that those expectations that we have tried so hard to comply with may not be true. We may have to admit that for once in our lives we have a whole lot more questions than answers. We feel powerless, alone, and don't know where to go or what to do. We discover the societal myth of success equaling happiness is bogus.

This "bottom" is a terrifying place to be and it's also a blessing! It may be a blessing in disguise, but it's a blessing nevertheless. In order to become authentic, each person needs to examine his current reality in depth in order to create a solid platform for building a new perspective on life and being at the bottom – suddenly realizing that everything you assumed to be true is questionable – is the perfect place to start. Many of my clients, when confronted with this "failure of success" paradox, become extremely agitated and angry. This is also good news! It hurts to be betrayed. It hurts to be misled. And it's difficult to accept that for all the struggling you've done, the keys to happiness were always within reach but out of your awareness. Being a serious professional may have served you well for survival into middle age, but beyond that it is literally a killer of your authenticity, your health and your closest relationships.

They don't teach you how to deal with the serious issues of stress, pressure and worry in grad school. On the contrary, they assume that these traits are supposed to be oozing out of serious professionals. After all, we are taught that no client/patient wants a happy, joyful, funny person dealing with important problems related to their well being. So here you are an established pillar of your community, back at square one in terms of your happiness and authenticity. It's enough to turn your hair gray, give you acid reflux, a bad back, chronic anxiety and who knows what else.

> **Your body is dying to talk to you.**

### *I Have Seen The Enemy*

*I have seen the enemy,*

*He is living inside*

*These walls that protect us*

*Where we thought we could hide.*

*I talk to the enemy*

*And he truly believes*

*He has fallen victim*

*To the liars and thieves.*

*I trusted the enemy,*

*He convinced me he's right.*

*He has shown me reasons*

*I should join in his fight.*

*We used to whisper about*

*Others not on our team*

*Then we left them behind*

*Now we need a new scheme.*

*I have seen the enemy.*

*The enemy is me.*

*It will be whoever*

*We decide it should be*

*Sharon Baird   November 2001*

## Getting Started: AWARENESS

The first leg of the journey to authenticity is **AWARENESS**. Since you have spent most of your adult life with your eye on a target, it's quite likely that you have failed to notice what is going on inside you. Often, the only clue that something is wrong is a vague inner discomfort. In my experience, it kind of sneaks up on you and has to get pretty uncomfortable before you even become aware of it. This, of course, is not how it is supposed to be. If you are a success, shouldn't you feel successful? So step one is becoming aware that, despite outward appearances, something inside you is telling you that your life is out of whack.

**Setting the Pace: REALITY**

The second leg on the journey to authenticity is **GETTING ACQUAINTED WITH REALITY.** You have become aware of the vague feeling inside you that something is not right. As you explore the feeling to find out what is behind it you will probably become aware that your spirit is getting smaller, that you're not having enough fun, and that you are not enjoying your hard-earned success. This is another one of those "simple but not easy" things. After all, you have spent most of your adult life trying to live up to someone else's story about how the world is supposed to be, so admitting that you don't feel successful (which is Reality) when you are supposed to feel successful (which is a Story about Reality) is a huge departure from your habitual way of being. Nevertheless, deep down inside, that's how you are really feeling. What a bummer! I don't recommend "happy pills" or visits to your local shrink. I suggest you allow yourself to really pay attention to whatever you feel about this critical time in your life; mad, sad, whatever. Shed some tears. Break some dishes. Let it out! It's a loss; it's a death. It's perfectly acceptable to grieve for those long years of effort and sacrifice and dehumanization.

A word of caution is appropriate here. You are about to go on an expedition to get acquainted with your own personal Reality and you are probably not going to like what you are going to discover. Don't fall into the trap of telling yourself a story about how much you are suffering. Feeling sorry for yourself is tempting because then you can act like a victim, get your friends to feel sorry for you, and avoid making the choice to do something different with your life. Don't use this as an excuse to assign blame. Blaming another person or circumstance for your pathetic state of affairs is just another convenient way of shifting the responsibility away from the only person who can really do anything about it. That would be <u>you</u>.

When you come right down to it, a prerequisite for recovering your authenticity is getting in touch with Reality. (Note that I've given Reality a capital "R." It's that important.) Ever since you were a kid, you have been trying to comply with somebody else's idea of how things – and you – <u>should</u> be. <u>Should</u> is not Reality; it's a <u>Story</u> about Reality. It's a fantasy. It's belief in a story from your parents, your teachers, your church and society in general about how they think the world should be. Once you have lost the ability to tell the difference between Reality and Stories about Reality, authenticity becomes impossible. How can you possibly be Real if you don't know what Real is?

> **If it doesn't kill you, it will make you stronger.**

One of the Stories about Reality you have bought into is that success equals happiness. The Reality is that you're not feeling happy; you feel miserable. Believing the Story "success equals happiness" is how you got into this mess in the first place. Isn't it amazing how you have learned to accept the Story as truth, pretend that the Reality of feeling miserable isn't real at all, AND THEN THINKING THERE IS SOMETHING WRONG WITH YOU BECAUSE YOU AUTHENTICALLY FEEL MISERABLE!! Believe it or not, that gnawing feeling of misery deep down inside you that you are so good at ignoring is right on the money. But you've learned to ignore it because you believe a Story that says it's not supposed to be that way.

If your current Reality is that you're miserable, so be it. Being miserable is neither good nor bad; it just is. Reality is just … interesting. The problem arises when you believe a <u>Story</u> about your current Reality. If your Reality is "I'm miserable" and your story is "I'm successful therefore I'm not supposed to be miserable," then the misery takes on the negative value of "badness." But the "badness" comes from the Story about the misery, not the Reality of the misery itself.

| Manure occurs! |
| --- |

Keeping a grip on Reality, like lots of other things in the journey toward authenticity, falls into the category of "simple but not easy." It's simple to understand the concept, but very difficult to apply it in the heat of battle. Why not think of it as a new skill to be learned rather than one more thing to screw up?

To help you get in touch with Reality, I'll propose some questions I use with my clients. It's a brainstorming technique. Take as long as you need with each item and then move on to the next one. Obviously, this could take some time. It's highly probable that you won't enjoy your answers. The task is to take an objective, dispassionate look at your professional and personal life with the emphasis being on Reality. The transition from being serious to being happy can only be based on a fearless inventory of your present Reality.

## QUESTIONS FOR GETTING REAL

Try a minimum of 10 responses to each question.
1) Who am I? (not what I do or a role that I play but the "real" me).
2) What do I want?
3) What do I need?
4) What do I pretend?
5) What makes me smile?
6) What makes me feel badly?
7) What 50 things have I always wanted to do but haven't had the time to do?
8) What rules do I need to change?
9) How can I manage time differently?
10) What's in the way of my choosing to be happy no matter what?
11) What role does fear play in my present life?
12) Who unconditionally loves me and why?
13) Who comforts me? Who can I really talk to?
14) What is the condition of my spirit these days?
15) What is my spiritual belief? (Not necessarily religious)
16) What is my belief about healing?
17) What is my belief regarding acceptance?
18) What is my belief regarding redemption?
19) Who knows or has known the authentic me?
20) What do I need to accept in myself so I can move on?
21) How does my faith or lack of it play into my current reality?
22) What do I believe in?

Congratulations on wading through this inventory! It takes courage to look in the mirror. Now that this soul searching process on your authenticity is completed and you've gotten a better handle on your current Reality, let's get with the third phase of the process. Let's move toward ACCEPTANCE as another crucial step to becoming real.

## Hitting Your Stride: ACCEPTANCE

ACCEPTANCE is the third leg of the journey and a critically important phenomenon that lies at the core of many of the concepts examined throughout this book. In the last section, you spent a lot of time learning about your personal Reality, so now you have a much better idea of what your Reality is. You also know that there is a lot more to your Reality than you suspected. At this point the question is – what is your relationship to this new Reality? How do you handle this new knowledge? To understand this and to get a better idea of what acceptance really is, it's helpful to look at the way our brains handle new information.

I have repeatedly made the point that the natural way of being for a child is to be open and curious. The main job of kids, especially young ones, is to get acquainted with a big, complicated world. Although children appear to be born with some response patterns hard-wired in the brain stem, (the "fight or flight" reaction, for instance) the vast majority of the response patterns we have at our disposal as adults are learned. Back in Chapter Two I proposed that the hidden agenda of the educational system is to turn the uncivilized little beasts called children into acceptable, functional adults. One aspect of that process is to teach children to respond in an appropriate manner to the situations they encounter every day.

Let's look at an example. Suppose a child is raised in a home with an abusive father and is subject to frequent beatings. As children, we magically believed that if something went wrong, it was our fault. "If I had been a better kid, then Dad wouldn't have beaten and punished me so much."

It's quite likely that the child might decide that in order to avoid punishment, an appropriate response would be to please Dad and anticipate Dad's every thought and action so he doesn't experience Dad's disapproval. The child makes up the Story that his job in life is to please people. Before long, a "pleasing people" habit is established and it becomes an automatic response. Unfortunately, pleasing people is an addictive disorder and is not compatible with authenticity.

Now let's look at your relationship to this little scenario through the lens of Reality. The kid in question was beaten by his father. What is your reaction to that? Take a minute and write it down.

> **Acceptance is the act of simply observing Reality as it happens.**

In reacting to this situation, most people respond with a Story about Reality. They respond with the particular Story they believe about child abuse. The reaction might be "it's awful that the little guy was beaten by his father. Nobody should be subjected to that. He probably grew up to be a sociopath and it was the rotten father's fault." Or they might think, "Kids are a pain in the neck. The little devil probably deserved it." The key point is that almost everyone bypasses Reality and automatically gets right to their Story about Reality. Leaving the Story about Reality out, what is the Reality here? It's simple. The kid was beaten by his father. That's Reality. Everything that comes after that is a Story. Acceptance is noticing what IS before reacting to it. There is a brief moment when it is possible to simply notice an event before reacting to it. That's where acceptance lives. (Be very aware here. Because of the automatic reactions that are hard-wired into you it's almost impossible not to let your stories about child abuse sneak in. And that's exactly the point. I am certainly not condoning – or condemning - child abuse, simply observing the Reality that it happened.)

Adults perceive themselves, other people and their current Reality through the lens of what should be rather than what is. As we struggle with the impossible task of being somebody, we distort and lose track of who we are, what other people are like, and we make life and death issues out of neutral Reality.

> **Acceptance is a key step in healing and becoming authentic.**

There is a biological price to be paid for being fear and anxiety based. As the years go by, the pursuit of serious professional life increases the stress we place upon ourselves. It's not just emotional wear and tear; there are also significant consequences to our physical well being. The stress becomes so pervasive that we think of it as normal. When we are under stress, our bodies produce adrenalin. Our caveman ancestors used adrenalin appropriately to survive the dangers of primal living. As working professionals, we use the chemical to get us through the anxiety and fear associated with our daily work life. As we ride the adrenalin high of the work week and the subsequent crash on weekends, we become addicted to this roller coaster of high and low feelings that this chemical reaction produces. This adrenalin haze makes it very difficult to accurately perceive ourselves, our relationships and our life situation. We think (or maybe don't think) in an entirely different way when adrenalin is in charge and the real problem is that we have come to believe that our adrenalin-mediated way of functioning is the way it should be. In a sense, we are addicted to the feelings produced by adrenalin. We have become "adrenalin junkies."

What's the problem with that? The caveman used adrenalin as a response to a perception of a life-and-death threat. The reaction happened and in the span of a few minutes it was over. As modern adults, we have somehow come to perceive "crabgrass on the lawn of life" as life-threatening. (Just watch the six o'clock news.) This chronic adrenalin reaction is an "oxidative" process. We literally "rust out" from the inside. We compromise our immune system, exhaust ourselves and dramatically increase the probability of serious illness.

The path of authenticity for the professional starts at the same place as the path of sobriety does for addicts. Acceptance of the fact that our lives are out of control puts us at "bottom." We must accept the fact that we are anxiety freaks or adrenalin junkies and are addicted to the frantic lifestyle of fulfilling other people's impossible expectations before we can make a clear choice for another way of life.

We talked about being hardwired for fear and anxiety in an earlier chapter. This is just anther name for adrenalin addiction. The good news is that this scenario can be changed with a simple (but not easy) choice. Choosing acceptance of our current Reality rather than the Story we have been using creates a new emotional and biological Reality to rewire. It's possible to generate new "wiring" by accepting yourself, others and your current Reality as it is. This choice provides us with a solid base to reshape our authentic life and "sober up."

I think it's safe to say that the more adrenalin dependent we become, the more we distort Reality. This phenomenon is true with any addiction. People in 12 step recovery programs call this process denial and it's exactly the opposite of acceptance. They could also call acceptance a synonym for sobriety.

People in denial have no perspective. They tend to maximize or minimize their Reality. Seeing others as larger than life or lower than whale poop, seeing yourself as a hero or a victim, and seeing your circumstances as rosy or disastrous is a hard way to go. Life truly becomes a soap opera.

> **The accurate diagnosis of an issue is as important as knowing how to fix it.**

Of course, the culprits in all of this denial are our old friends WORTHLESS and SOMETHING AWFUL IS GOING TO HAPPEN. These two powerful messages rear their ugly heads when the person in denial is under pressure or stress. Adrenalin junkies love a challenge, thrive on chaos, and savor crisis, and then they inevitably crash.

We have all heard about PTSD (post traumatic stress disorder), which was called battle fatigue in the old days. I believe that my adrenalin addicted clients suffer from the same illness as our troops in the Middle East. The difference is that our soldiers are truly in life threatening situations every day, while we attach a life-and-death response to an imagined threat. The brain does not discriminate between real life-and-death situations and imagined ones. While the soldier could be blown away at any moment, we are adrenalized by a patient missing an appointment or a staff member coming back late from lunch.

By choosing authenticity, by accepting who you are as well as your current Reality, you are in a sense choosing sobriety. In recovery programs, one of the most powerful tools is a simple prayer: *God grant me serenity to accept the things I cannot change, the courage to change the things I can, and the wisdom to know the difference.* Authenticity requires courage, acceptance and wisdom. That's what acceptance and the choice of real authenticity is all about.

Here's another way to look at acceptance. Self worth, by definition, is the ability to give and receive unconditional acceptance (love). This means I accept myself, others and my Reality AS IS.

> **It is as useful to know who does not love you as to know who does.**

Most of us have been loved and accepted with conditions. I'll love you IF you're a good boy or girl. I'll love you IF you're getting good grades. I'll love you IF you win the game. I'll love you IF you star in the play. I'll love you IF you get a scholarship. I'll REALLY love you IF you become a doctor. If there is an IF in the equation, it's not true acceptance.

> **If you want to learn about unconditional love, get a puppy.**

Unconditional acceptance is a gift that is rarely given in our society. I can count on one hand the times I have experienced unconditional acceptance. Conditional acceptance is often manipulative and inauthentic. Those who have never been given unconditional love themselves are incapable of giving what they haven't experienced. Most of us wanted unconditional love from our parents and we blamed them if we didn't get it. We sometimes hold people responsible for being perfect, loving parents when in Reality, all they can do is the best they can. Sad but true.

Theoretically, a marriage/partnership should be the easiest opportunity to show unconditional love, however, knowing someone intimately doesn't guarantee a built-in path to acceptance. The challenges of living with someone day in and day out, squeezing the toothpaste tube from the top (bottom), leaving the toilet seat up (down), and arguing over the checkbook seem to dim the glow of pure unconditionality. My wife and I both struggle with being unconditionally loving 24/7 so this next expression of her love is particularly meaningful to me.

### ***The Gift You Give***

*I acknowledged my gratitude to you once*

*at an Emeritus meeting*

*for seeing who I am,*

*for knowing and accepting "ME".*

*Not always liking what you see*

*But accepting nonetheless.*

*That is the gift you give*

*to others you engage with –*

*Isaac, Roger, Larry, Dave, Kyle, Sharon –*

*I could go on…. and on.*

*That is a rare gift.*

*Thank you,*

*Others may not thank you.*
*Some may flee, terrified, and hide,*
*but the ones who are ready to know*
*that having someone see them*
*is a gift that is priceless.*

*Your spousal unit*
*Barbara Campbell*

Love/acceptance begins with you. By focusing on being authentic you will experience the feelings of unconditional acceptance that you missed out on as a child. This, in turn, will allow you to be comfortable in your own skin, give you the ability to unconditionally accept others, and allow you to make authentic choices in the here and now. Simple? Yes. Easy? No.

One last analogy: acceptance is like a vision screening. First, you must become aware that you're not seeing very clearly. Once you stop feeling sorry for yourself and decide to do something about it, you pick up the phone and schedule an eye exam. After the exam, the prescription might be Lasik surgery or, more likely, new lenses to clear up your vision. Then, as if by magic, the world that had been a blur appears in sharp focus and you're seeing clearly. Think of acceptance as admitting you aren't seeing your current Reality very clearly. You accept feeling stuck, discontented, worried, and scared. The choice of accepting your Reality is the key step in seeing clearly and by choosing new, authentic lenses you are able to see the world without distortion, fear or anxiety. See what I mean?

What does acceptance feel like? Perhaps it's better to explore what it doesn't feel like because we are all more familiar with those feelings. Acceptance does <u>not</u> feel like anger, resentment, fear, shame, guilt, envy, anxiety, disgust, the need to be perfect or the need to be in control. It does not feel like dependence, pressure or blame. Acceptance <u>does</u> feel peaceful and serene. Acceptance puts the seat of power within us rather than outside.

## Heading for Home: GRATITUDE

The fourth leg on the journey to authenticity is GRATITUDE. Some people call this beautiful phenomenon appreciation, but I prefer gratitude. Being grateful

> **Gratitude is the currency of healing.**

is more than just showing appreciation. Appreciation is about approval and admiration but gratitude shows that you have been touched deeply and that you are thankful. Appreciation is something you have but gratitude is something you give back to the world. There is an element of vulnerability in gratitude. Showing people that you

> **If you don't love yourself, no one else will.**

acknowledge, feel, and allow life's precious moments is what makes the authentic leader even more powerful and approachable. I've found that expressing my gratitude has opened up some very unexpected avenues for me and my clients. When I express gratitude for even one of the many gifts and blessings I have, it automatically broadens my context. All of a sudden, what's right about life gets included and things that seemed like life and death issues or insurmountable barriers turn into mere crabgrass on the lawn of life.

There's another thing about gratitude that is almost unbelievable. Way back in Chapter Two, I casually mentioned that the misery we feel is fear-based. Understanding – and experiencing - this concept is critically important and this is a good opportunity to explore it a bit further. We have noted that, when you get to the bottom of things, there are really only two basic fears. One is "I am not enough" and/or "I do not have enough." The second basic fear is "something awful is going to happen." The "something awful" may be a specific thing or event, or it may be a non-specific feeling of dread.

I have repeatedly made the point that we lost our authenticity and the joy fizzled out when we stopped being ourselves and began to try to be "somebody". We began to try to live up to somebody else's Story about how we SHOULD be. Further, it happened when we were just kids. We've lived our entire adult lives in an unnatural state of misery. What in the world would keep us doing that? One of the two basic fears! We live by some variation of one of these two stories: "I can't be myself because my real, natural self is WORTHLESS" or "If I don't act the way I'm supposed to, SOMETHING AWFUL IS GOING TO HAPPEN."

Amazingly, modern brain scanning techniques have demonstrated that the circuits and hormones that are activated during the fear reaction are quieted and replaced by a whole different set of reactions when we feel gratitude. The bottom line is this: IT'S IMPOSSIBLE TO BE FEARFUL AND GRATEFUL

> **Gratitude is the antidote to fear.**

AT THE SAME TIME! To illustrate why, I suggest that my clients make a list (in case you haven't noticed, I'm big on lists) of all the people in their life that they are grateful for. After each name, make a note listing what it is about them that contributes positively to your life. Now find a quiet place to sit. Concentrate on your breathing, allowing it to become slow and regular for a few minutes. Now pick one thing on the list and think about it. Lose yourself in it. As you do, pay attention to the internal state of your body. Notice your "gut feeling." You'll find it's more peaceful than usual. As you go deeper into this gratitude meditation, note that your sense of serenity increases.

What you have just accomplished is simple enough to do, but it is really a minor miracle. You have actually CHOSEN to activate a positive physiologic response that is the opposite of the fear response. A few paragraphs ago, we made the point that the fear response rusts you out from the inside. The response you have just chosen does exactly the opposite. It's restorative. It's a positive, healing state of being. And it is available to you by choice. The tragedy is that this state, which was so readily available that it was our natural state as children, is unfamiliar to us as responsible grownups. Let's look at some examples to see how it's possible to recapture our natural ability to choose gratitude and experience that healing state.

> **Your health is directly correlated to your peace of mind.**

The following poem was given to me after a session on authenticity that I conducted with Dave's team. To me, it is a perfect expression of gratitude.

## *Whisper*

*Like a whisper can fill a concert hall*
*Waiting for the music to start.*
*It takes just one thought to fill many minds.*
*With the hope of touching one heart.*

*Like a feather that drifts from a mountain*
*After lifting an eagle in flight.*
*It takes just one key to open the cage*
*Of a spirit sheltered from light.*

*Like a black cloud carried the needed rain,*
*Feeds the world when the gardens grow,*
*It takes just one willing teacher to share*
*The seeds of their knowledge to sow.*

*You don't have to be an almighty god*
*To fill the hearts of the hollow.*
*It takes just one whisper to start the song,*
*And soon the others will follow.*

*You have chosen to live as a teacher,*
*To the Universe, that seems small,*

*But to those who are searching for answers,*

*Your whisper is heard by us all.*

*Sharon Baird   July 2006*

*Dedicated to Dr. Bill Campbell on his 65th birthday*

Sharon's expression of gratitude led me to pick up my quill and parchment and, as if by magic, the following poem appeared on an ink-splattered page.

### **The "Live" Poets Society**

*She doesn't really write poetry.*

*She is poetry.*

*The words come from places that few of us experience.*

*Places of the heart and gut where only the brave go.*

*Her writing has an edge.*

*The rhymes are an inside-out process*

*that touches my authenticity.*

*If it's true that life imitates art*

*then her art is a mirror for me to find*

*that authentic place where only real stuff dwells.*

*I suppose you could call it a gift, a talent, a drive*

*or even an obsession, but*

*I call it a "work in progress."*

*After all*

*That's all any of us can attempt:*

*To make our lives an authentic work of art.*

*Bill Campbell    February 2008*

The next letter from my grandson, Griffin, age 9, is an example of gratitude from a child's perspective. It is not as poetic and elegant as Sharon's adult expression and the spelling is a little shaky, but it's just as authentic and validating.

> **Gratitude and fear are mutually exclusive.**

*Dear Grandpa,*

*I am thankful for you because you are silly and love to spend time with me. For example, one time my friend, my grandpa and I were golfing at my grandpa's course. He spotted a dead gardener snake smashed out on the cart path. So my grandpa decided to put it in my brother's golf bag. When we got back to the house, we immediately went to the back of Mom's car and sniffed the dead rotting passenger in my brother's golf bag.*

*After my brother found the snake he was furios and wanted revenge. So the next time we visited grandpa, my brother set the alarm clock next to his bed for 3 o'clock in the morning. My grandpa said it was horrible and he got no sleep.*

*My grandpa loves to tell me funny jokes and likes to give me grief. He loves to spend time with my brother and I, he takes us to movies and to go golfing a lot because he lives next to a course.*

*I am so thankful for my grandpa. He is a very specail person. He comes to all my sports games. He is funny, kind and sweet and I am thankful to have him as my grandpa.*

*Love, Griffin*

I'm grateful to my grandson for his unabashed authenticity. It is effortless for him to tell me how much he loves me and why. For the natural child, the expression of authentic affection is natural and normal. In my own personal experience, it's amazing how one person's authentic expression of gratitude awakens the almost primal authentic response of affection that we were so easily able to feel before we became "somebody."

# CHAPTER 4: ELEMENTS OF AUTHENTICITY

It seems almost silly to dedicate a whole book to the notion that the key to becoming a great leader is to become real. For most of my professional life, I've been looking for the holy grail of leadership and it's been under my very nose all that time. I won't say that I'm the sharpest pencil in the box but like most professional folks, I thought the answers to effective leadership were all outside of myself in the realm of knowledge, skills and techniques. Over time, I have come to realize that it wasn't the skill set of the leader that made the difference; it was only the depth of his authenticity.

This simple discovery is not quite as simple as it sounds because what I have discovered is that there are some commonalities that authentic leaders share and these common principles transcend knowledge, skills and techniques. These principles are profound and take time and effort to understand, but I do believe that old dogs <u>can</u> learn new tricks. So, let's examine these elements.

## 1) AUTHENTICITY IS NOT A LEARNED OR ACQUIRED TRAIT. IT IS A MATTER OF AWARENESS AND CHOICE.

In the process of trying to be somebody, we lose our natural tendencies and become serious, responsible adults. The "somebody" we try so hard to become is created by the expectations of others. Our natural, childlike human qualities are not lost forever, however. They are still imprinted in the pathways of our brains. The problem, as we have seen, is that we have been hard-wired to believe that our authentic self is somehow wrong, inappropriate or even shameful. A common example of how this works is the injunction that it's not acceptable for a male to express any emotions, other than anger, in public. If you watch little boys before they have started on the path to being somebody, you'll discover that they cry several times a day. What happens to those emotions in adulthood? We have bought into the story that "real men don't cry" so when a situation arises where tears are a perfectly appropriate response, we bottle it up and try to hide it. We try to pretend that the authentic response (tears) doesn't even exist. In fact, it's likely that we work up some shame about even feeling the emotion. This "denial of emotion" response pattern that men develop as a way of learning to control the tears becomes a habit. Although we can't remember doing it, at some point in our childhood we made the unconscious choice to be a "real man."

> **Feelings are a temporary physiological/chemical event.**

If we have the ability to choose not to cry, we also have the ability to make a different, more authentic choice. The emotions are real. Is there any reason not to honor them except the cultural message that "real men don't cry?"

"Real men don't cry" was my Story about Reality. Awareness and acceptance of the inauthenticity of the Story have given me the option of choosing a different response. I now tend to shed tears when I'm touched deeply in any human way. In my macho-psychotic years, I would allow myself to cry in a movie where in that dark environment nobody could see my humanity, but that was about it. Now I'm apt to cry at the drop of a hat, and it feels so natural to express those most human emotions of sadness, joy, surprise, or whatever I'm feeling at the time.

> **We all choose to feel the way we do. We are in total charge of how we choose to express those feelings.**

So in a very real sense, authenticity is an inside-out proposition. It comes from the basic decision to <u>choose</u> to be ourselves; to <u>allow</u> ourselves to <u>be</u> who we are rather than to always <u>do</u> what we think we are supposed to do. It comes from having the courage to be real, spontaneous and to allow what is inside of us to see the light of day. The key word here is <u>choice</u>. In the example I've used, choosing to be human and allow access to true feelings demonstrates one real strength of the authentic leader.

## 2) AUTHENTICITY IS SIMPLE BUT NOT EASY

All the decisions you made as a kid that robbed you of your authenticity (I'm worthless. Something awful is going to happen. I can't afford that. I have to be serious to be successful. Men don't cry, etc.) are now hard-wired into your brain. They are connected to the fear reaction, so all the ugly chemical results that go with the fear reaction are part of your response. In short, you are hard-wired to feel lousy and rust out from the inside. That's why you might be successful but you don't feel successful.

There's one more thing. All this hard-wiring took place when you were a kid. The brain of a child is very plastic and easily programmed. It has to be because that's when you learned an astonishing amount of very complex stuff (like language, what the world is like and how to behave in it) in a very short time. By the time you were well into your teens, your ability to hard-wire new circuits had diminished significantly and the older you get, the harder it becomes. In order to reclaim your lost authenticity, you have to rewire those circuits as a grown-up professional with a brain that is not as plastic as it was when you wired it in the first place.

So, what does it mean that it's simple but not easy? It's simple to understand the process that got you to where you are today. It makes logical sense. It's about ideas and concepts and you are good at grasping those sorts of things. But it's not the ideas and concepts that make you feel miserable. It's the automatic, hard-wired <u>responses</u>. And they are very difficult to change. It's simple to understand the process but it's not easy to change the response. You don't reclaim the child in you by learning how you lost it. You reclaim the child in you by being aware of your inner feelings and emotions and learning to choose a different response – and that's not easy! It requires that you do some new hard-wiring in an old brain. The goal is to learn to recognize when you are trapped in the fear response and be able to choose a different, more appropriate one.

> **It's not the problem that gets you in trouble. It's your hard-wired response.**

## 3) CHOOSING HAPPINESS IS THE EXPRESSION OF AUTHENTICITY

While pursuing this notion of authenticity, I came across a revolutionary idea: Happiness is <u>not</u> an occasional special experience. <u>It is a choice!</u> It is a learnable skill. It's where the rubber meets the road in an authentic life.

Happiness had always seemed like a result to me. Happiness was a fleeting feeling I got to experience for a job well done, a special moment in a relationship or as a brief reflection of a life-long accomplishment. Happiness was illusive, serendipitous, short term, all too infrequent and always dependent on some situation, person or circumstance outside of myself.

My serious, professional self had always regarded happy people as being somewhat silly, Pollyannaish, and to be truthful, not very bright. After all, in this miserable, pain ridden world we all inhabit, how can a person be happy all of the time? They must not be paying attention. Doesn't any responsible

> **All the stuff in the world is not enough to make you happy.**

adult know that suffering is what respectable serious adults are supposed to do? That's what I thought, but how wrong I was!!

Choosing to be happy, no matter what, is one of the most important ingredients for authenticity. Being happy

> **Pain is mandatory, suffering is optional.**

no matter what does <u>not</u> mean that you ignore rough times, terrible losses, or problems to be solved. Painful events happen as part of the human condition. It's part of Reality. Being happy no matter what <u>does</u> mean

51

that suffering is optional and that your mindset can be happy no matter what the circumstances are in your life. It's a matter of consciously giving up the Story about Reality that people, situations, things or circumstance can make you happy. The trophy wife (or husband), the McMansion, the plastic surgery and the Rolex might be the trappings of success, but they are the myths of happiness.

The analogy here is that thin people process food differently than fat people. Happy people process the things that happen to them differently than miserable people. Recent studies have shown that happy, positive, proactive people use their brain differently, have different chemistry in their bodies, and have fewer symptoms of chronic stress and disease than unhappy, negative, fear-based folks.

Happy people refuse to be victimized by anything in life. They realize that we may not always be able to choose what cards are dealt to us, but we can darn well choose how we play them. Happy people are also very aware that we always have a choice of how we react in any given situation. The freedom to choose

> You can't be victimized without your permission.

is what enables us to be happy and authentic in the long run.

## 4) ACCOUNTABILITY IS THE LANGUAGE OF REALITY

Authentic people are accountable for their actions, their state of mind and their communication. They do not assign blame; they do not throw anyone under the bus, and they take total responsibility for their choices. If something goes south, they evaluate the current reality, weigh the options and make a corrective decision. Because of this, they do not have regrets about what they have done in the past, tend to be fearless about making mistakes, and accept whatever the future might bring. Their focus is on the here and now and what can be learned from the decisions they make. In short, they trust themselves; they trust their employees; they assign little credit or blame for results. Most of all, they are accountable for the quality of their lives.

> **If you don't like the decision you made, make another one.**

Serious professionals often have the mentality of "staying the course," "sticking to the game plan," "a card laid is a card played." Authentic leaders, on the other hand, are not afraid to change their mind, their direction or to tweak an already successful formula. If something doesn't work, they make another decision followed by curiosity and wonder what will happen next.

# CHAPTER 5: HOW DO AUTHENTIC LEADERS BEHAVE?

By watching my clients, friends and occasionally even myself over the years, I have observed that authentic leaders act differently than others. Here are some of the behaviors that seem to be central to authenticity in the business setting.

## 1) AUTHENTIC LEADERS HAVE A STRONG VISION ABOUT THEIR BUSINESS

I work very hard with my clients to create a clear and sensory rich image of the future of the business. When a person becomes authentic rather than "professional," a fundamental shift in behavior occurs. Instead of reacting to situations as they occur and "reinventing the wheel" in response to every crisis, they begin to proactively move in the direction of their ideal future. Some of them choose to build a new facility or remodel an existing office to match their vision of what the image should look like. Others change their basic business structure or reconfigure their staff.

Let me share some examples. One client in Florida had an office that was painfully conventional. When he chose authenticity, he decided that his office should reflect his love of the beautiful seaside location of his practice and should represent his passion for boating and fishing. He commissioned an artist to cover the walls from floor to ceiling with murals of local waterfront scenes. He gathered his collection of nautical artifacts and turned them into decorative accents. Fishing poles became curtain rods. Fishnets became room dividers. Now his office is authentic. It portrays his love of the location and life on the water. When you walk into his office, you are clearly in a seaside environment, where his enjoyment of his work matches the fun of the beach.

Another client shared a large, family-oriented dental practice with a colleague in the nation's capital. He was financially successful, but hated to come to work every day because of negative confrontational encounters with his partner and doing the "boring, one tooth dentistry" that he dreaded. Once he accepted the Reality that he and his partner were not compatible and that his office space was too large for a single practice, he chose to create a new future for himself. His new vision motivated him to move his office across the hall into a space half the size, to "divorce" his partner, and to develop a compact, small-staffed, boutique-style restorative practice that reflects his true passion: a natural love of cosmetic treatment. His fear was that something awful would happen; that the change would dramatically reduce his income and lead to financial disaster. (He actually had an image in his mind of selling pencils on the sidewalk outside his old office.) His fear-based Story about Reality turned out to be bogus. In Reality, the authentic changes he made have been wildly successful – both economically and for his personal happiness.

Another client was a 60 year old who had worked in the same small, cramped office for 27 years. He was becoming less and less motivated by his career and had resigned himself to "sticking it out" until he could retire. As he slowly emerged from his self-imposed emotional imprisonment and became aware of his natural, authentic self, he decided to take an uncharacteristic risk. He chose to "escape" by expanding his office as well as his spirit. The transformation took a full year, but he weathered the inconvenience and challenges of the construction process. His vision of a space that honored his late father sustained him throughout the process. His new office is like a small temple with subtle décor and is an exquisite expression of his Japanese roots. Beautiful orchids, a passion of his late father, are the thematic connection to his past and the serenity that choosing happiness has created. He expressed it in poetry like this:

### _A Very Short Story About a Very, Very Long Journey_

_Once upon a time, the mystical child reached out with his hand to the authentic self and said, "I want to take you on my journey."_

_The authentic self said, "I cannot go with you because I am trapped in my wound."_

_The child could only watch, and had to choose to conform or to rebel. Once the choice was made, the journey was lonely and fraught with danger. The child occasionally got a glimpse of the authentic self, but could not make a connection. This would go on for years._

_Then one day, the authentic self received a gift. The gift was the opportunity to heal the wound._

_The process was difficult and painful, but with time and the help of many sages the authentic self said, "ENOUGH!"_

*The authentic self reclaimed the key that opened the door to healing. Those responsible for the wound were held accountable for their actions and the healing began.*

*As the door opened, the mystical child could be seen waiting for the authentic self. The child smiled and clasped hands with the authentic self, and the journey began anew.*

*Dr. Art Yamasaki*

These examples show how authentic leaders tend to express their spirit in the design and presentation of their environments. Their surroundings are symbolic of the things that mean so much to them. Not only do these practices deliver wonderful professional service, they also mirror the authentic selves of those leaders who spend so much of their lives in that environment.

There is another dimension to an authentic environment beside the physical design of the office. The emotional environment is every bit as significant as the bricks and mortar. Another one of my clients who has transformed himself into an authentic leader took an unprecedented risk in the pursuit of "happiness no matter what." As he became increasingly authentic and therefore increasingly happy, he became aware that sustaining his own happiness in an inauthentic emotional environment was impossible. Some of his long-term employees were too fear-based to join him on his journey. He tried a number of interventions to change the awareness level of these people. The results were mixed. It seemed like "the rich got richer and the poor got poorer." While some responded positively, the inauthentic team members only escalated their unhappiness, blame and soap opera behavior.

The leader became aware that the actors in the soap opera were an increasing roadblock on the office's journey to happiness. So he had three choices: 1) He could continue his efforts to change the dysfunctional behavior. 2) He could work on his tolerance for the shenanigans, or 3) He could "clean house." These are all difficult choices. Some of the offenders had been part of the team for decades and played an important role in the success of the business. They were lovable people with some very annoying hard-wired behaviors. It seemed that they were unconsciously choosing to perpetuate the soap opera. He was able to accept them as people but unable to accept their behavior. It was impossible for him to extend unconditional acceptance to them and that became a crisis of his own authenticity. In other words, "I will love you if . . ." became the problem. The leader suffered over this dilemma for many months. It seemed like it was a "no win" situation. On one hand, he loved these people. On the other, they were the biggest stumbling blocks to his vision of an authentic workplace.

> **Vision without action is a pipedream. Action without vision is wheel spinning. Vision plus action can change the world.**

So following the principles of this book, he made a decision based on his own "gut feelings." This was new behavior for him and required that he face the fear that something awful was going to happen and that he would lose the love of these people. After he gathered his

> **Leadership is about changing the rules, not about attempting to change people.**

courage and made the uncomfortable decision to sever his professional relationship with them, the business has flourished and he has a smile on his face. His vision of a happy workplace, no matter what, gave him the courage him to make the tough decisions he would not have otherwise been willing to make.

## 2) THE MISSION STATEMENT

From 12 year old students at Stanley British Primary School, Denver, CO:

*"In our homeroom, we are all individuals, but we stand together as a team. We want our homeroom to be a place where it is safe to express ourselves and to voice our opinions, questions, and feelings. We want it to be a place where everyone is included, appreciated and supported.*

*"To make our vision a reality, we will respect each other. We will come to class each day with positive attitudes. We will be inclusive, kind, and selfless. We will be ourselves. Lastly, we will make time for balance in our lives; we know we have time for fun, time to learn, and time to look out for and take care of each other."*

The mission statement is another important piece of the authenticity pie. A mission should present a clear picture to the leader, staff and clients as to the <u>purpose</u> of the business. I believe mission statements should be short and inspiring. They should announce the values of the leader and the people involved in the business.

The act of articulating a vision for your business and writing a mission statement is an important step on the road to authenticity. The early years of a business are usually spent in "survival" mode. Not only is the fledgling leader of the business busy trying to be someone else, he's also trying to make enough money to feed his family, pay off his debts, and impress his colleagues. He's not proactive, but reactive to every situation that comes along. Ironically, the business reflects exactly who the leader is; it's just that he has never consciously thought about who he is.

This is not to say that a young professional doesn't plan the kind of business he or she wants to have. But in the early years, the vision involves "doing." If you ask a young person about to start a business to write a vision, they will tell you what they want to be "doing" in five or ten years. The journey to authenticity begins when the vision shifts to answers the question, "Who am I?" and the business comes to be a conscious effort to integrate who you are with what you do.

I'm a big fan of having a business vision and mission statement and rewriting them on a regular basis. It's instructive to see how the vision evolves along with the leader and how the act of writing the vision is a tool for self-awareness. As an example of the mission statement reflecting the evolution of the leader/team, let's look at the mission statement of an actual business. A decade ago their mission statement was "Quality dentistry for a lifetime." This illustrates the awareness level of the organization at the time. They were aware of the connection between quality professional service and building a lifetime relationship with their patients. Not bad, but hardly inspiring. There is just as much fear of losing a patient implicit in this message as the promise of an authentic relationship.

Fast-forward to the present. The mission statement now reads "The right dentistry for real people by real people." In my opinion, this statement demonstrates a great deal of growth and evolution of the venture. It introduces the notion of "rightness" which says to me "appropriate treatment" and honesty. It also acknowledges the authenticity of both the patient and the care providers. This mission statement is not a story about fear-based dentistry. It speaks to a higher level of awareness; the notion that all parties involved in this relationship are reality-based and are valuable human beings.

## 3) AUTHENTIC LEADERS HAVE LOW TOLERANCE FOR CHAOS AND AMBIGUITY

Before we look at the reasons for this, it's helpful to define what we mean by chaos and ambiguity. Ambiguity comes from the failure of the leader to paint a clear picture of who he is and what he wants. Chaos is the confusion that results from this lack of clarity. Some of this ambiguity disease is a side-effect of the busy brain of a professional who is trying very hard to survive and be somebody. Some of it comes from the leader's failure to understand who he is. But the biggest cause of chaos is fear – fear of survival, fear of making a mistake, fear of offending a client/patient, fear of offending a staff member, fear of confronting unacceptable behavior, fear that something awful is going to happen, but most of all, fear that the world will find out that deep down inside the leader is worthless. After all, how can a leader be clear about how he wants his staff to behave if he is not even clear that he is worthwhile enough to be the leader? As a matter of fact, inauthentic leaders cause most of the chaos and ambiguity in their offices, and then blame it on circumstances or the staff. Since the leader can't see the real cause of the problem, he can't understand that the solution does not lie in altering the staff or the circumstances. It's within himself. I suggest he might want to check himself into "Ambiguity and Chaos Anonymous."

There's another cause of chaos that I've observed time and time again in the offices of my clients and that is the "drama queen" (or king.) These are people who are naturally emotionally noisy. They need to be the center of attention and they need to create emotional upheaval. These people are toxic because they are addicted to chaos and will sabotage the healthy, peaceful atmosphere that is the hallmark of an authentic environment. If you have a lot of soap opera disorder in your office, then you are guilty of allowing ambiguity to dominate the culture of your practice. An authentic leader will confront this sort of behavior and do whatever is necessary to eliminate it.

Authentic leaders are inclined to stomp out ambiguity with a vengeance. Because they are not tolerant of chaos, they are aggressive about making decisions that lead to clarity and serenity. Making clear rules, having clear procedures and creating

> **It's very difficult to have more than three rules for yourself or your team. KISS!**

consequences for violators are natural byproducts of authenticity. Dare to make it simple and easy!

Before you interpret the last paragraph to mean that you should run a tight, dictatorial ship, consider a couple of subtle but important concepts. First is that an authentic leader is firm in principle but flexible in practice. Here's what I mean: On a trip through rural Scotland several years ago, I came around a bend in the road to find a farmer waving at me to stop. He had a small, black and white border collie with him and was next to a pasture containing several hundred sheep. Once traffic was stopped, he opened the gate and let the sheep out on the road. It was his intent to move them to another fenced pasture several hundred yards away. Once the sheep got out, they started off in all directions. The farmer did nothing, but the collie went to work. He circled the herd and started moving them in the right direction. Whenever a few sheep set out on their own, the dog circled around them and moved them back into the herd. Before long, all the sheep had gone through the open gate of the new pasture.

The point is this: There was a lot of apparent confusion within the herd. Sheep do not march in file with military precision, they mill around in all directions. It didn't matter to the collie (or the farmer, for that matter) that within the herd some of the sheep were headed in a different direction than others. What mattered was that the herd as a whole was on the right track and that in the end, everybody got where they were supposed to go. That's the way an authentic leader operates. He defines the direction and makes sure that his team is headed there. Not everyone on the team gets from point A to point B along exactly the same path, and that's fine because the authentic leader honors each team member's unique way of being. But if somebody gets too far off track, it's the leader's job to herd them back in or remove them from the team.

In addition to presenting a clear vision about where the business is going, authentic leaders eliminate ambiguity by presenting a clear picture of where the practice is at the present moment. It's like getting directions on Mapquest. You need to know where you want to go, but you also need to know where you are starting from before you can begin the journey. This is not as easy as it seems, because defining present Reality is difficult for a leader who is also the chief cook and bottle washer. If the leader is also the main producer, he must be focused on production if the business is to thrive. If his attention is on the client and production, it's NOT on the behind-the-scenes soap opera that is going on in the office. Additionally, a small business usually cannot afford a manager/human resource person whose job it is to know what is going on and deal with it. One of my main jobs as a consultant is to evaluate the problems that occur in my clients' organizations and present them to the leader so that the leader knows where to start. Even if the leader does know what is going on, defining present reality might very well lead to confrontation of inappropriate behaviors on the part of a team member, a job that few leaders relish.

Change, or even the prospect of change, takes people out of their comfort zone. Note that it is NOT the job of the authentic leader to make everyone comfortable. In fact, if the main focus of the leader is making everybody happy, it's a virtual certainty that there's no authenticity in the process.

## 4) AUTHENTIC LEADERS ARE FLEXIBLE

There's a maxim in the world of sports that says "champions adjust." That means true champions have the ability to adapt their strategy to the circumstances of the game. Serious professionals, on the other hand, often have the mentality of "sticking to the game plan" "winners never quit" or "quitters never win." Authentic

> **You always have choices, no matter what.**

leaders are open to outcomes and are not afraid to change their minds. That is not to say that if things go wrong they abandon their vision and go off in a different direction. There's an old saying that if you don't know where you're going, any road will take you there. For authentic leaders, it's exactly the opposite. They clearly know where they are going but are not attached to one specific way of getting there.

## 5) AUTHENTIC LEADERS CREATE CHALLENGES

This last topic related to authentic business is pretty obvious to an outside observer, but not at all obvious to the leader. It takes a great deal of awareness and courage to choose happiness and authenticity for yourself and your organization. It's a significant change and some of your staff will not be on the band wagon, at least in the beginning. In my experience, because there is no real opportunity to climb the corporate ladder in a small venture, people channel the energy they would use in vertical ambition in a large organizational environment to creating disruptions in the small private setting. Often the leader is the one who becomes the focus of negative attention. It seems to be human nature to view the leader as the one responsible for everyone's bad feelings, the target of blame, and the person to fight with or to criticize. If you are not a strong leader, you <u>will</u> become the target for all of the ills of the office.

A strategy I have developed over the years is to have leaders provide challenges for themselves and their staffs so that negativity doesn't have time to gestate. A positive way to create this challenge is to establish the expectation that there is always something to be learned. If you create a culture where people are learning things that keep them slightly out of their comfort zone, good things always happen. Training and development is the key to inspiring and retaining a great staff. Each person in your office, including you, should have a development plan that increases each individual's skill and worth to the practice. This plan should be consistent with your vision and should make everyone better prepared for the challenge your vision creates for the future.

The authentic professional's vision should determine the needs of the organization in the future and the impediments to achieving that future should become the challenge. For example, one big future challenge of being in a small business will be to attract enough new clients to maintain cash flow in a hostile economic environment. In order to get enough people through the door, the key area of training and development is marketing. Learning how to find new clients who understand and value your vision of service will allow you to have an authentic and successful practice.

The path of least resistance is to want training and development in the areas you already have competency. The problem is that people who are trying to be somebody usually want more of what they already have rather than what they really need. For example, the temptation in a professional practice is to focus on training in technical procedures, which will have little effect on the happiness level of the business, rather than on personal growth issues which, although uncomfortable, might lead to significant change. It takes some uncommon vision, clarity and authenticity to create a focused development plan that will do your small business the most good. If authenticity is your goal then you, out of necessity, must learn to think out of the box, get outside your comfort zone and go beyond conventional wisdom for your answers. We are trained in our profession, not as salespeople or marketing experts. The courage to rise to this challenge could make or break your business.

# CHAPTER 6: AUTHENTICITY IS SIMPLE BUT NOT EASY

Authenticity means living your own life on your own terms. It's a simple concept but not easy! The difficulty is that there is no cookbook recipe for your unique style of authenticity. That's a good news/bad news thing. The strategies we have talked about throughout this book are all valid and have worked for my clients. But because there's nobody else exactly like you and there's no other path to authenticity exactly like yours, you have to find a way to make the journey that is uniquely your own. Because it is an inside out process, the strategies and tactics for an authentic business have to come from your imagination and your untapped creativity.

You have survived until now on fear and compliance to the expectations of others. You will thrive if you allow your own gifts to emerge and have some fun with the journey. The hall-of-fame football coach, Vince Lombardi, said many years ago that winning is not everything; it's the only thing. I couldn't disagree more! For me, it's the willingness to play <u>your</u> game that is both the only thing and everything.

Willingness to participate in the game of life is what is important to the authentic person. Winning and losing are completely defined by the player, not by a preconceived scoring system. As a matter of fact, losing isn't in the equation of the authentic leader because his self-worth is not tied to outcomes. The winning formula is: Am I happy? Am I having fun? Am I creating a business that serves people well and makes a difference?

> **Knowledge without action is just talk. Action without knowledge treats symptoms. Knowledge plus action equals success.**

One of the benefits of learning is the ability to make a change in behavior. I don't believe that authenticity can be learned in the conventional sense. It's based on a part of you that already exists somewhere down there in the deep recesses of your soul. It just needs to be liberated/chosen/allowed. In previous chapters in this book, I've described some fundamental principles of authenticity. Each of these fundamentals is a choice. Living in the precious present is a choice. Being grateful, accountable, happy and accepting are certainly choices, and when you add all these choice points together, you get transformation.

Transformation is not gradual, incremental change. Transformation means a structural change across boundaries. I strongly believe that a person can be miserable, stuck, depressed, lonely, empty and full of despair one moment, and be on the journey to authenticity in the next. In the long run, the freedom to exercise our powers of choice is what makes us human "beings."

> **It's never about you.**

So, what would your life feel like if you experienced the transformation to authenticity? What I can tell you is based on my experience with the numbers of people I have encountered over many years on this journey. And I do think that I have experienced many of these choices and resulting transformational phenomena for myself.

Authentic persons just plain enjoy life more than folks who are desperately trying to be somebody. Choosing to be happy no matter what seems to change the thought process and the physiology of folks who go that route. I see more smiles, more belly laughs, more humor, more energy, and more access to feelings. In short, I see a more present, available person who is in touch with himself, and who is grateful to be where he is on the journey.

I also see less rigidity, more flexibility, more creativity, and a greater willingness to experiment. I see big changes in relationships because people are accepted for who they really are, not as someone to judge or to "fix." I see men become more open and honest with their feelings. I see women become less anxious about pleasing everyone on the planet. Probably the biggest difference I see and hear from this transformation is that worry is not an issue anymore. Food tastes better; sex is more than just a physical release. It's like the fog has lifted and they can see the world in HD, surround sound, and in vivid, living color.

I know that this sounds very magical, almost like a religious experience. You can call it what you choose. All I know is that we all have so much spirit in our humanity that it's a simple choice to live that spiritual energy rather than be dragged down by the troubles of the planet. Having your emotions tied to the fluctuations in the stock market, the winning or losing of your NFL team, your golf handicap, or the cash flow in your business sucks the life out of you. Living your authentic life without measures is a much more fulfilling way to be.

I've seen some remarkable changes in the way businesses are run. Authentic businesses have a whole different feel than a corporate or franchise atmosphere. When a business reflects the personal energy of the leader, when the staff has caught the "authenticity bug," and when your clients feel that they belong to something very special, real magic can occur.

Transformational energy is very different from survival energy. Survival has a desperate, frantic, fearful, negative charge because everything is about life and death, therefore everything is self serving and everything is about "me." Authentic leaders and practices run on an entirely different wavelength. When your business engine runs on happiness, fun, enjoyment, celebration of self, and being human, the focus is not about life and death. It's about expression. It's about your authentic Self, not your ego. It's about community, not isolation. It's about health, not disease. It's about solutions, not problems. It's about what we can accomplish together, not about me fixing you. It's a celebration, a paradigm shift, fusion of past and future in the present. It's like the movie *Back to the Future*.

I can't guarantee that authenticity will raise your bottom line, allow you to send your kids to Harvard or let you buy all the new toys that the media says you must have in order to be successful. My guarantee runs something like this: If you will do your homework, i.e. go through the steps of admitting your failure of success, feeling the loss, getting a grip on Reality, accepting yourself, and then being grateful for the journey and all you do have in life...if you do all that, I <u>guarantee</u> that your life will be sweeter and you will have a solid base to choose an authentic life from now on, whatever that might look like.

I can't guarantee that you'll be taller, smarter, or sexier. I can guarantee that you will be a great deal more lovable and happy if you allow people to see the real you.

# CHAPTER 7: THE FORMULA FOR CHANGE

I have chosen the path of authenticity:

- If I choose to do something about the issues in my life rather than worry about them.
- If I choose peace of mind over obsessing about my weaknesses and perceived shortcomings.
- If I choose happiness over being stuck and miserable.
- If I choose to live in the here and now rather than dwell on the past or worry about the future.
- If I learn to deal with my natural instincts rather than to over-think everything.
- If I choose to view my professional life as fun rather than work.
- If I choose to define my life as enjoyable rather than life-and-death serious.
- If I choose to relearn how to play.
- If I spend my reflective time on gratitude rather than what's wrong with my life.
- If I learn to relax even in stressful moments.
- If I choose to take responsibility for my life rather than blame someone else for my current situation.
- If I consistently choose love rather than fear.
- If I choose to believe in a power greater than myself.
- If I choose to focus on life one day at a time.

- If I choose to allow unconditional love into my life rather than loneliness and isolation.
- If I choose to receive as well as give.
- If I choose to enjoy myself when circumstances seem dire.
- If I choose to live my life as a human being rather than a human doing.
- If I choose to lead by example rather than by teaching and preaching.
- If I learn to let go rather than control.
- If I choose to view my past as merely a context for decision making in the present.
- If I choose to view people's mistakes (including my own) as an opportunity to learn rather than character flaws.
- If I choose to respond authentically to people rather than give in to my addiction of people pleasing.
- If I choose to believe the idea that people love me (or not) for who I am rather than what I do for them.
- If I choose personal power over victimization.
- If I choose to focus on wealth (quality of life) rather than riches (stuff of life).
- If I choose to listen rather than enlighten.
- If I choose to embrace life's challenges rather than fear them.
- If I choose to take care of my own spirit rather than delegating that chore to another person or organization.
- If I choose to love people (including myself) for who they are rather than whom I want them to be.
- If I practice self-acceptance in all things, especially my past.

- If I realize that the past is over and the only thing I have control over is how I choose to view the present.
- If I choose to keep it simple, honest and open.
- If I choose to refrain from trying to change people.
- If I remember that most people need acceptance, not help.
- Finally, if I choose to take some risks, lighten up and have some fun, and learn to count my blessings, I'll be just fine.

Let me leave you with my version of the AA prayer:

### The Authenticity Prayer

God grant me the serenity that comes from
the ability to perceive Reality,
The courage to choose to be happy no matter what,
And the wisdom to accept myself as I am.

# Epilogue:
# An Authenticity Primer

This last section is a collection of ideas, aphorisms, random thoughts, questions and one-liners that formed the rough outline for this book. Dave and I gathered this material from a decade of consulting, seminars and coaching with our client/professionals. These pages are not intended to read like a book, however, the real meat of our thesis is contained in this unconventional format. We hope that studying these thoughts will allow you to develop a context for your own unique style of authenticity. Some of this material appeared previously in the text, but we feel that it is important enough to warrant repetition.

## 1) PRINCIPLES OF AUTHENTICITY or WHAT YOU DIDN'T LEARN IN SCHOOL

- The most useful things that I have learned didn't come from the classroom.
- Your perception is your reality.
- Meaning is context dependent.
- Placing blame is a waste of time and energy.
- Rich means having money. Wealth is a quality of life. All the "stuff" in the world is not enough to make you happy.
- Self worth is the ability to give and receive unconditional love.

- Success is getting what you want. Happiness is wanting what you get.
- There is no such thing as a mistake; there is only learning.
- There is nothing as important as being in the here and now.
- There is no <u>one</u> way to do anything.
- Remember that most people are fear-based. Bravado and arrogance are covers for a basically scared person.
- Gratitude and fear are mutually exclusive.
- You can't be victimized without your permission.
- The fundamental choice is to be happy, no matter what.
- Feelings are a temporary physiological/chemical event.
- Trying to avoid risk and adversity is folly. Learning to deal with adversity as Reality is authentic.
- You can tell the quality of a person by who loves him and who doesn't.
- The secret to true happiness is to lower your expectations.
- Learning is the ability to change your behavior.
- You don't need to change yourself or work on your perceived weaknesses. Take what you've got and make it better.
- All suffering is self inflicted.
- Victimhood is based on the idea that you don't have a choice.
- The diagnosis of an issue is as important as knowing how to fix it.
- If it doesn't kill you, it will make you stronger.
- Authentic action is power.
- You always have choices, no matter what!

- When you change your behavior, you increase your number of choices.
- Authenticity is an inside-out process.
- What is authentic for one person may not be for another.
- Our society does not reward authenticity.
- Fear and love are mutually exclusive.
- The need to please people and authenticity are mutually exclusive.
- Kindness and authenticity are not the same thing, but can comfortably co-exist.
- Authenticity is simple but not easy.

## 2) THE AUTHENTIC PERSON

- If you don't love yourself, no one else will.
- It's never about you.
- You never learn anything when you are talking.
- It's impossible to be tense and relaxed at the same time.
- You are not what you do.
- You are not your image.
- If you need someone's approval, you give away your power to them.
- Personal power comes with the commitment to authenticity.
- You are as good as your habits.
- Acceptance is a key step in healing and becoming authentic.
- It's as useful to know who does not love you as to know who does.
- You can't give away what you have not experienced.

- If you want to learn about unconditional love, buy a puppy.
- Your body is dying to talk to you.
- Worry is the 8th deadly sin.
- Champions adjust.
- If you focus on your limitations and listen to constructive criticism you will always sabotage yourself.
- We all choose to feel the way we do. We are in total charge of how we choose to express those feelings.
- If you want to understand another person, pay attention to your gut feelings.
- Children can be your greatest teachers if you'll stop trying the "raise" them and learn to listen.
- Your health is directly correlated to your peace of mind.
- Your happiness is directly correlated to authenticity.
- Your happiness is directly correlated to your peace of mind.
- It's difficult to be non-judgmental. It's how you deal with those judgments that counts.
- The need to please people is an addiction.
- Accepting yourself for who you really are is the first step in unconditional love.
- A stiff upper lip breaks down with real adversity.
- Raising authentic children may be your biggest contribution and gift to the world.
- Being of authentic service to people is your earthly purpose for being.
- Real compassion comes from a hard-nosed attitude about reality.
- Being hardnosed and kind are not mutually exclusive.
- Being nice in order to be liked is incompatible with authenticity.

## 3) THE AUTHENTIC LEADER

- Being a leader is an honor, not a position.
- You can't have the same expectations for males and females. We are different animals.
- Women lead differently than men because of their brain physiology and experience.
- Gender politics has nothing to do with Reality.
- Authenticity leads to realistic expectations for your team.
- Real leaders are always seeking congruence.
- If you are willing to "be", people will follow your vision.
- Ineffective leaders try to influence people to go to places the leader hasn't experienced.
- Our society needs authentic leaders.
- There is no one authentic leadership style that is better than any other.
- The definition of crazy is doing the same thing over and over and expecting different results. *(borrowed from A. Einstein)*
- Love beats fear every time.
- It's very difficult to have more than three rules for yourself or your team. KISS.
- Leadership is about changing the rules, not about attempting to change people.
- Education. Experience. Talent. You need two out of three to meet the conventional expectation of success. Authenticity creates its own brand of success.
- Learning when to shut up and listen is an important skill for an authentic leader.
- Vision without action is a pipedream. Action without vision is wheel spinning. Vision plus action can change the world.

- Learn as many jokes as you can about your profession. You never know when they might come in handy.
- Treat everyone as if they were your client.
- The service you deliver is not nearly as important as how you take care of your client.
- The biggest challenge in a small business is hiring authentic people.
- You don't have the time, resources, or training to manage your team. Hire talented, authentic people who are self starters.
- Small businesses generally run more like a family than a corporation.
- Many of the skills that managers in corporations covet do not apply to leaders of a small business.
- There is a huge difference between management and leadership.
- Hiring people that make you "comfortable" is <u>not</u> an authentic strategy.
- Hiring real grown-ups <u>is</u> an authentic strategy.
- Diversity in the workplace is not about race or gender; it's about diversity of perception and thought.
- Your clients don't necessarily have to like you, but it helps.
- If it isn't fun, you'll burn out in the long haul.
- Talent is critical in hiring. Happiness is a talent.
- Your job as a leader is to hold the vision, stomp out ambiguity and develop yourself and your team based on the vision.

## 4) THE AUTHENTIC BUSINESS

- The most successful businesses are a reflection of the authentic self of the leader.

- Teams allow leaders to lead; it's not a God-given right.
- An excellent team shares the vision and commits to it.
- The quality of feedback determines the performance of the team.
- Knowing how to support the vision of the leader is more important than leadership itself.
- A brilliant vision leads nowhere without commitment.
- Authenticity is more important for outstanding performance than skill and experience.
- Sharing the same vision makes it possible for the team and the leader to be in the same boat.
- Conflict can come from individual visions that collide.
- Conflict is one symptom of the leader's inability to provide an inspiring and purposeful vision.
- Ambiguity can lead to conflict and dysfunction.
- A small business that becomes too comfortable, too efficient and too routine in its operation is a breeding ground for negativity.
- Authentic businesses seek challenges and embrace the discomfort of discovery.
- The creative process keeps everyone engaged and passionate.

## 5) EVERY AUTHENTIC LEADER NEEDS AUTHENTIC FOLLOWERS

- Remember who signs your paycheck.
- Remember whose business it is.
- Loyalty is a mixed bag; there's a fine line between unconditional love and dependence.
- If you're not growing as a team, you're going backwards.
- Team goals are more important than your goals.

- If your goals are incompatible with the team vision, why are you on the team?
- Play to your strengths; ask for help with your weaknesses.
- Give input on new hires; you have to work with them day in and day out.
- Make sure you were hired for your talents and that you remain employed for those gifts.
- Be grateful for what your teammates bring to the organization.
- Be proud of who you are and how you got there.
- Be grateful for an emotionally safe workplace; most folks have no place to escape from the chaos in their lives.
- The quality of a team is best measured by the quality of the feedback given to one another.
- Treat your teammates as if they were your clients/patients.
- Treat your leader as if he was your client/patient.
- No matter what it says on the door, your real business is your clients/patients; try to walk in their shoes.
- Pick an organization that fits your authentic style. Don't try to fit in. Your job in an interview is to learn if this situation fits you, not the other way around.
- You can be valuable to an organization as team player. You can be equally valuable as an individual contributor. The real question is - which role makes you happy?
- Employees are most happy when their personal style coincides with the organizational style.
- Talk to your leader about creating a development plan so you can help him fulfill the mission of the organization with your new skills.

- Whether yours is an authentic business or a work in progress, remember that your leader is struggling with the challenge of his own authenticity. Practice acceptance and be grateful that you are a part of a unique journey.

## FINAL EXAM

You don't have to cram, review your notes or stay up all night worrying about your grade on this final exam. Your teachers don't give rip about your score. Just take the exam and have some fun with it. It just might tell you something about yourself!

1. Pick the three concepts that are most important to you.

| | |
|---|---|
| ___ acceptance | ___ happiness |
| ___ wealth | ___ unconditional love |
| ___ peace of mind | ___ congruity |
| ___ enjoyment | ___ friendship |
| ___ leadership | ___ acknowledgment |
| ___ financial security | ___ choice |

2. What 3 ideas worked best for you in this book?

3. Explain: authenticity is simple but not easy.

4. What concept in authenticity was the most difficult for you?

5. What was the key decision you made as a child that led you to become a serious professional?

6. Explain the "failure of success" as it applies to you.

7. What concept of becoming an authentic leader is most challenging for you?

8. On a scale of 1 to 10, how hopeful are you about your ability and commitment to becoming authentic? Why?

9. List the relationships in your life that are not authentic. What can you do about them?

10. Are these concepts revolutionary to you or have you known this stuff all along?

11. What prevents you from becoming authentic?

12. What are your behavioral addictions? What behavioral addictions are you attracted to in others?

13. What do you need to stop doing to be authentic?

14. What do you need to start doing to be authentic?

15. What do you need to continue doing to be authentic?

16. Is your business a reflection of your authenticity? If not, why not?

17. Write your own epitaph.

18. Name the authentic leaders in your life. Why are they authentic?

19. What behaviors from your authentic role models would you like to imitate?

20. How would "happy no matter what" transform your life?

I would like to express my gratitude to:

Dave Nibouar – Sage, dentist, editor and spiritual advisor.
Sharon Baird – Poet Laureate, Limestone Dental Associates.
Griffin Callahan – Grandson, student athlete, authentic kid.
Barbara Campbell – Spousal unit, support system, editor.
Art Yamasaki – Haiku specialist, taiko drum aficionado, road racer, authentic procrastinator.
Jim McKelvey - Dentist emeritus, joke collector and distributor, organ transplant recipient, wooden boat builder.

## RESOURCES

What Happy People Know by Dan Baker
Taming Your Gremlin by Richard D. Carson
What Could He Be Thinking? by Michael Gurian
The Path of Least Resistance by Robert Fritz
The Way of the Peaceful Warrior by Dan Millman
Wild at Heart by John Eldridge
The Little Book of the Shadow by Robert Bly
A Christmas Carol by Charles Dickens
The Vein of Gold by Julia Cameron

The authors are available to consult with your small business or professional practice and to speak or facilitate meetings and retreats. To contact Bill or Dave:
- Dr. Bill Campbell: campbell.wb@comcast.net
- Dr. Dave Nibouar: ratcatcherfarm@verizon.net